Vegan Bodybuilding;
A Scientific Workout Regime with the Ultimate Vegan Diet, Building a Great Physique with Vegan Food, Vegan Bodybuilder Workout, Vegan Diet Plan, Vegan Weight Training, Vegan Nutrition
By
M Laurence

Table of Contents

1. The Plan to Build the Body

The RIGHT vegan diet plus the RIGHT bodybuilding regime EQUALS rock-hard quality muscle. There is absolutely no reason at all for a vegan diet to restrict anyone in the slightest when it comes to packing on muscle.

Vegan Bodybuilding is becoming more popular day by day but it is still the core basics that matter – consuming the correct calorific intake to allow muscle growth and the correct weight training to break the muscles down ready for that growth.

I have developed a hard-hitting workout regime geared toward utilising a powerhouse Nutrient-dense Vegan Diet combined with a Scientific-based Weights workout. This constituted a lot of research looking at the most effective exercises that generated the maximum muscle response.

For example I would now always start my Biceps workout with a Chin Up and then Seated Curls. These two are the most powerful muscle activators. I honed down the most effective exercises into a simple easy-to-follow plan for maximum results.

The archetype of traditional meat-eating bodybuilding is now being turned on its head when it comes to muscle building. Going meat-free doesn't mean you can't pack on rock hard muscle or achieve your fitness goals. Instead, science is showing us that eating a plant-based diet might be one of the best ways to not only live a healthy life but might also allow you to reach your goals faster.

Now many professional bodybuilders are vegan bodybuilders and have developed strong, ripped physiques while eating only plant-based foods.

If you're a looking to build lean muscle hy way of a vegan bodybuilding diet, this book is the ideal resource you need to get started.

To give you a quick overview of how we will achieve this I have broken the training regime down into 3 areas:

1 - Training Frequency

Many people say you can only train a body part once a week. This is theory is outdated. As usual all we have to do is look to the past. Did you know many of the 60's and 70's bodybuilders were training the entire body 2-3 times a week. 3 times a week is extreme for a normal person who has to work and earn a living etc But we will make sure we work hard.

The weight training plan is high-impact, time-efficient and results-driven. I wanted a heavy duty '2 week workout' plan that I could simply repeat which added enough variation week to week to keep the muscles guessing and therefore keep growing.

Week 1

I wanted big compound movements in week 1 to drive size, growth and boast Testosterone. Compound moves burn more calories throughout your workout, because more muscles are working. They allow you to get a full-body workout in less time. Core strength will also be improved as something like a Squat will recruit more of your muscles to work synergistically compared to say a Leg Extension which will work your Quads.

Week 2

Week 2 including some of the compounds moves but focused on specific body parts such as Shoulders, Arms and Calves so nothing was left behind.

2 - Body Fat

There's a number of things you need to consider to get the maximum out of your workouts. Your Testosterone is utilized at its best when you have a lower body fat percentage. So this is the number one issue to deal with when beginning a new regime. A low body fat percentage gives you more utilization.

3 - Nutrition

Nutrition is considered the most important part of building muscle and with our Vegan lifestyle we need to be somewhat more specific. If the nutrition is incorrect, Vegan or not, then it doesn't matter how impeccable your training routines are, you will not progress. I'm sure you have an idea about nutrition, but I'm here to give your knowledge a little boast. You've heard of high protein, carbohydrates and healthy fats? But what is the most effective foods to eat to get those essential nutrients?

We need to feed your muscles exactly what they need and therefore you will build muscle. Last but not least is a high water intake, this cleans our systems, regulates body temperature and keeps the entire body hydrated. So with heavy exercise, 3 litres a day is an ideal figure to aim for.

2. The Science Behind Growth

Week 1 Compound

So as I've already said this is a two week workout splitting the Upper and Lower body up. And repeat. Week 1 you will train the whole body twice in 4 workouts, 2 lower and 2 upper. This will shock the muscles into growth. The additional work-load will blast the muscles into adjusting and therefore grow. We will certainly have rest days and rest Sunday.

The second week reverts to training the whole body once in smaller more precision based workouts. This will utilise supersets to keep our workouts intense and time-efficient. This will keep your muscles guessing from the previous week. Nothing stunts growth like the same workout week in week out.

Science-Back Exercises

I've researched many studies to hone down the precise exercises that make more impact that others on muscle growth. It stands to reason that not all exercises are equal, but which ones are best?

Let's take Chest for example. The best exercise according to numerous studies (including Contreras, PhD, CSCS EMG Study) are Incline Dumbbell Bench Press. This has the greatest ROM (range of motion) which is directly attributed to building muscle. It is also extremely effective at activating the upper chest. Finally because you're using dumbbells you are forcing each arm, each pec to perform equally and not rely on a stronger side. Next would be flat bench as studies are shown there is a direct correlation to the 1 x Rep Max you can lift and the size of your chest. So we want to put that next. Also depending on your musculature, you may find doing this with Dumbbells and not a barbell because in some cases the shoulders end up being activated more than you would want.

I've gone through each bodypart, looking at previous research and cutting edge techniques, and compiled this into a list for what is the best and most effective exercises for growth and symmetry.

Supersets to Size

Supersets are time-efficient will be used in Week 2. By doing sets back-to-back, you reduce your total workout time while still doing the same amount of total work. Supersetting is fantastic for pummelling antagonistic muscles - Back/Chest and Biceps/Triceps and legs Hams/Glutes. Supersets increase Lactic Acid production, which helps boost Growth Hormone (GH) levels in the body. The body responds to the reduced pH (increased acidity) in the body from the production of Lactic Acid by secreting GH. GH is a powerful fat loss and muscle building hormone.

Power and Intensity

We will be building more explosive power which will therefore build strength faster. This is done using tempo. By this I mean a 1 second pull/push/ on a given move - POWERFUL and with FORCE - and then under perfect control a 4 second release. The muscles are still working all the way. So we are changing the tempo, the speed of either the concentric (shortening) or eccentric (lengthening) component of the lift. There is no 'resting' at the bottom of any move. As soon as you are as close to the bottom of the move - you POWER back up for the 1 second concentric and again release for 4 second eccentric under your complete control. This should give you a great pump and be a big challenge to start with.

Why the time?

You must have heard of the term TUT - Time Under Tension - there are a number of variations on the term, they all mean the same. You may find that you're actually only working your muscles for 5 minutes in an hour workout! With the 1 second concentric and 4 second eccentric move with no rest we work the muscle much harder for longer.

Many people will struggle with this at first as it's so common to do one arm curl, take a break/release all tension and do another. Even a split second rest is still a release of tension. Not good enough. You need to be working your muscles 100% of the time during a set. THEN you rest between sets. You will do more damage to the muscle and get better results to stimulate growth.

3. Before You Begin

Make sure you are in good health to begin with. See a Doctor if need be to make sure you are okay to begin training.

Some of these exercises for example the Bulgarian Split Squat maybe the first time you are doing them. I would for the first 2 weeks go light on the weight. Certainly lighter than normal. I want you to go back and really feel the muscle working. When researching this book and completing these exercises I went back to light weights, back to when I started training.

The difference was startling. I had got used to using heavy weight and wasn't feeling that exact muscle contracting, almost starting down that pointless road of beginning to use body momentum, not thinking about the specific exercise and losing that edge of concentration.

Using light weight made me think about how each muscle was working all over again. Now I feel revitalised. I took a step back, did the research, made each and every exercise and rep count. Even performing light Squats and Romanian Deadlifts were like new moves. Now with my Diet and new weight regime I'm making giant strides forward and enjoying every single workout.

Let's get to it.

4. Monday - LOWER

Weights:
I like my heavy workout first thing in the morning. If this is the case for you as well you need fuel before you go, something fast digesting: a 25gram protein shake, a banana and a handful of granola prior to a workout.

The exercises are one after the other. Rest time is 45 seconds per set. So at 30 seconds the weights should be back in your hand. Keep water with a scoop of BCAA's handy.

Always warm up before any training. Do a 5 Minute walk and jog on the running machine. Do bodyweight squats, make sure your shoulders and neck are warmed up.

Increase the weight little by little with each set.

Exercise	Sets/Reps
SQUAT	1-2 sets of 15 reps (warm-up); 5 sets of 12, 10, 8, 6, 4 reps
ROMANIAN DEADLIFT	5 sets of 12, 10, 8, 6, 4 reps

BULGARIAN SPLIT SQUAT	3 sets of 12, 12, 12
HAMSTRING CURL	4 sets of 12, 12, 10, 10

STANDING SINGLE LEG CALVE RAISE	4 sets of 12, 12, 10, 10

SEATED CALVE RAISE	3 sets of 12, 12, 12

5. Monday - Nutrition

We are aiming for the widely accepted figure 1 gram of protein for 1 pound of body weight to give your muscles the fuel to grow. For example:

A person weighing 176bls / 80kg you would aim for 176grams of protein.

This is relatively high. However protein shakes can add easy grams of protein to your diet. Now this is a guide. You might try this and after a few weeks feel you're not getting enough. In which case you could add a further 50 grams of protein to your diet through two smaller meals, an extra protein shake or simply making your meals a little larger. Some nutritionists even recommend 1-2 grams of protein to 1 pound of bodyweight.
So the person weighing 176 would eat between 176 (1.5grams of protein) and 353 (2 grams of protein)

The emphasis is on continuous supply of nutrients - protein and fat. Carbs are placed at the start of the day - in among your training ideally. You ideally don't want any carbs after lunch.

Ultimately you will have to experiment, see how your body reacts. If you weigh 176lbs don't try and eat 353 grams of protein straight away, start at the lower end of the spectrum. Phase your body into this, let it adjust. So let's get to it.

Meal One

1 x multivitamin

Oats and Fresh Fruit
- 1/4 cup Quinoa oats with 1 tbsp. honey – use Almond Milk.
- Add blueberries and half a banana for a more filling and sweeter taste.

NUTRITION FACTS
Calories: 460   Fat: 10.4 g Carbs: 46.2 g Protein: 15.1 g

Meal Two

Lean Shake
- 2 Scoops of 25 gram per scoop of Pea Protein Isolate.
- For a lean shake use water or mix with ½ cup of almond milk.

NUTRITION FACTS
Calories: 230   Fat: 20 g   Carbs: 10 g   Protein: 50 g

Meal Three

Stir fried Tofu with vegetables
- Smoked Vegan Tofu stir fried with your favourite vegetables.
- Try red, green and yellow bell peppers, carrots, broccoli and cabbage for a hearty colourful selection.

NUTRITION FACTS
Calories: 438   Fat: 29 g   Carbs: 43 g   Protein: 28 g

Meal Four

Butternut squash and chick pea curry
- Add coconut milk to your curry paste and then cook the vegetables and allow to simmer
- Boil ¼ cup of brown rice
- Sprinkle some toasted almonds and cashews on top and serve (2 ounces).

NUTRITION FACTS
Calories: 452   Fat: 34 g Carb: 18 g   Protein: 32 g

The Total Protein intake is 125.1 grams of protein. I would have 2 scoops of protein after your workout, plus Creatine making a grand total of 175.1.

This is a figure you can play with, add more Tofu in the stir fry or make a double portion and have the second one later. Adversely if you feel bloated, reduce the intake for a week etc

6. Tuesday - Cardio

Our legs will be sore so we don't need to do anything too extreme. I like to rest the muscles between weights days. Swimming would be fantastic, realistically walking 50 minutes. If you want then you can do a 20-25 minute run.

Cardio - A.M
Before breakfast go for a 25minute run. This burns fat straightaway and gets your metabolism fired up.

7. Tuesday - Nutrition

Meal One

1 x multivitamin

1 x Whey Protein shake - with peanut butter and a banana

1 x Bowl of Granola

NUTRITION FACTS
Calories: 361   Fat: 18.4 g Carbs: 30.2 g Protein: 32.5 g

Meal Two

Lean Shake
- Add 2 Scoops of a 25 gram protein Whey Isolate to ½ cup of almond milk or water.
- Try adding a spoon of flax seeds for added nutrition.

NUTRITION FACTS
Calories: 230   Fat: 20 g   Carbs: 10 g   Protein: 50 g

Meal Three

Pea Soup
- Peas are boiled and blended with celery and vegetable stock sprinkled with vegan cheese.

NUTRITION FACTS
Calories: 271   Fat: 13.2 g   Carbs: 17 g   Protein: 18 g

Meal Four

Veggie Chilli
- Make your chilli using soy mince or Quorn mince adding lentils and kidney beans.

NUTRITION FACTS
Calories: 452   Fat: 14 g Carb: 18 g   Protein: 26 g

The Total Protein intake is 126.5 grams of protein. I would have 2 scoops of protein plus Creatine after your workout making a grand total of 176.5.

This is a figure you can play with, add more, take away some etc

8. Wednesday - UPPER

With the other workouts i superset two moves and this saves time and creates a cardio effect, while allowing you to hit two body parts hard. However with legs which are a very large body part and demand heavy workouts I do one exercise at a time. Also remember your limits with heavy weight. It is much better to master your form for Squats with a lighter weight. Let your muscles get used to the heavy weight gradually.

Cardio - A.M
Before breakfast go for a 25minute run. This burns fat straightaway and gets your metabolism fired up.

Weights:
Again if training first thing: a 25gram protein shake, a banana and a handful of granola prior to a workout. If you do weights first thing in the morning move your cardio to before dinner.

Rest time is 45 seconds per set. So at 30 seconds the weights should be back in your hand.

WORKOUT

Increase the weight little by little with each set.

Exercise	Sets/Reps
INCLINE DUMBELL PRESS	1-2 sets of 15 reps (warm-up); 5 sets of 12, 10, 8, 6, 4 reps
CHEST SUPPORTED ROW	5 sets of 15, 12, 10, 8, 8 reps
OVERHEAD PRESS	4 sets of 10 reps

PULL UP	4 sets of 10 reps
INCLINE DUMBELL CURLS	4 sets of 12, 10, 8, 8 reps
LYING DUMBELL TRICEPS EXTENSION	4 sets of 12, 10, 8, 8 reps

LATERAL RAISE	4 sets of 12, 10, 8, 8 reps
PRESS UPS	1 Set to Failure
BENT OVER BARBELL ROW	1 Set to Failure

9. Wednesday - Nutrition

Meal One

- 3-4 Whole Eggs Boiled
- 2 Quorn sausages

Quinoa or gluten free oats
- 1/4 cup of oats with 1 tbsp. honey

NUTRITION FACTS
Calories: 361   Fat: 24.4 g   Carbs: 36.2 g   Protein: 36.1 g

Meal Two

- 2 Scoops of 25 gram Pea protein powder mixed with ½ cup of almond milk

NUTRITION FACTS
Calories: 230   Fat: 20 g   Carbs: 10 g   Protein: 50 g

Meal Three

Pulses Salad Bowl
- Add Green salad leaves (try kale, spinach, rocket)
- Top with lentils, beans, pine nuts, peanut butter and vegan cheese.

NUTRITION FACTS
Calories: 471   Fat: 33.2 g   Carbs: 17 g   Protein: 18 g

Meal Four

Vegan Spinach Lasagne
- Use vegan cheese, organic spinach and serve with a side salad of fresh green leaves topped with balsamic vinegar

NUTRITION FACTS
Calories: 452   Fat: 34 g Carb: 38 g   Protein: 27 g

The Total Protein intake is 131.1 grams of protein. I would have 2 scoops of protein after your workout making a grand total of 181.1.

This is a figure you can play with, add more, take away some etc.

10. Thursday - Cardio

Okay we will be going for a little cardio today. If you don't feel like running because you're sore, then walk 50 minutes, swim. Something that is cardio-based.

Cardio - A.M
Before breakfast go for a 25minute run. This burns fat straightaway and gets your metabolism fired up.

11. Thursday - Nutrition

Meal One

1 x multivitamin

6 x Scrambled Whole Eggs.
* Add a dash of lemon juice, and pinch of black pepper for taste.

Gluten free porridge oats
* 1/4 cup with 1 tbsp. honey
* Add chopped banana

NUTRITION FACTS
Calories: 461   Fat: 30.4 g   Carbs: 46.2 g   Protein: 40.1g

Meal Two

Protein shake
* 2 Scoops of 25 gram protein Whey Isolate
* Add Almond milk or water

NUTRITION FACTS
Calories: 230   Fat: 20 g   Carbs: 10 g   Protein: 50 g

Meal Three

Vegan Fajita's
* Stir fry smoked tofu with black beans and green peppers
* Wrap using corn tortillas
* Sprinkle with vegan cheese
* Add tomato salsa and guacamole

NUTRITION FACTS
Calories: 471   Fat: 13.2 g   Carbs: 27 g   Protein: 28 g

Meal Four

Tofu steak and vegetables
- High protein Tofu steak grilled or BBQ
- Serve with brown rice or Quinoa
- Steam Broccoli and Cauliflower

NUTRITION FACTS
Calories: 452   Fat: 24 g Carb: 28 g   Protein: 22 g

The Total Protein intake is 140.1 grams of protein. I would have 2 scoops of protein plus creatine after your workout making a grand total of 190.1.

This is a figure you can play with, add more, take away some etc.

12. Friday - LOWER

This being the second workout of the week we are hitting different muscles and attacking them using less sets.

Cardio - A.M
Before breakfast go for a 25minute run. This burns fat straightaway and gets your metabolism fired up.

Weights:
Morning workout: a 25gram protein shake, a banana and a handful of granola prior to a workout. If you do weights first thing in the morning move your cardio to before dinner.

Exercise	Sets/Reps
SQUAT	1-2 sets of 15 reps (warm-up); 5 sets of 12, 10, 8, 6, 4 reps
ROMANIAN DEADLIFT	5 sets of 12, 10, 8, 6, 4 reps

BULGARIAN SPLIT SQUAT	3 sets of 12, 12, 12
HAMSTRING CURL	4 sets of 12, 12, 10, 10

STANDING SINGLE LEG CALVE RAISE	4 sets of 12, 12, 10, 10
SEATED CALVE RAISE	3 sets of 12, 12, 12

13. Friday - Nutrition

Meal One

1 x multivitamin

Egg and Spinach Omelette
- 3-4 Whole Eggs whisked with a handful of organic spinach leaved loosely chopped and added to omelette
- Serve on a bed of fresh lettuce leaves (the greener the better)

Gluten Free Granola
- Granola with almond milk. Add fresh fruit and honey to taste.

NUTRITION FACTS
Calories: 461   Fat: 30.4 g Carbs: 16.2 g Protein: 34.1 g

Meal Two

Protein Shake
- 2 Scoops of 25 gram pea protein added to 1/2cup of water.
- Add a few cubes of ice, almond milk and banana for a more substantial snack.

NUTRITION FACTS
Calories: 230   Fat: 20 g Carbs: 10 g   Protein: 50 g

Meal Three

Beetroot Salad with Tofu pieces
- Add beetroot sliced on a bed of green leaves
- Add cooked quinoa on top
- Slice some tofu pieces

- Crumble some vegan cheese
- Sprinkle some roast pine nuts

Treat

As a treat have a plant based or natural seeded protein bar. Try 'Nutrimino' for a high protein snack.

NUTRITION FACTS

Calories: 471   Fat: 33.2 g   Carbs: 17 g   Protein: 26 g

Meal Four

Vegan Sausage and Mash
- Grill 4 vegan sausages
- Boil and mash x2 small sweet potatoes and serve

NUTRITION FACTS

Calories: 552   Fat: 34 g Carb: 18 g   Protein: 27 g

The Total Protein intake is 137.1 grams of protein. I would have 2 scoops of protein plus creatine after your workout making a grand total of 187.1.

This is a figure you can play with, add more, take away some etc.

14. Saturday - UPPER

Here is the second workout of the week, still hard and heavy but less sets. The legs will have recovered since the last workout and now need another hit. But by reducing the amount of sets they will be ready for the next workout which is bigger.

Cardio - A.M
Before breakfast go for a 25minute run. This burns fat straightaway and gets your metabolism fired up.

Weights:
The exercises are split into two exercises per round performed one set after another. Rest time is 45 seconds per set. So at 30 seconds the weights should be back in your hand.

WORKOUT

Increase the weight little by little with each set.

Exercise	Sets/Reps
INCLINE DUMBELL PRESS	1-2 sets of 15 reps (warm-up); 5 sets of 12, 10, 8, 6, 4 reps
CHEST SUPPORTED ROW	5 sets of 15, 12, 10, 8, 8 reps
OVERHEAD PRESS	4 sets of 10 reps

PULL UP	4 sets of 10 reps
INCLINE DUMBELL CURLS	4 sets of 12, 10, 8, 8 reps
LYING DUMBELL TRICEPS EXTENSION	4 sets of 12, 10, 8, 8 reps

LATERAL RAISE	4 sets of 12, 10, 8, 8 reps
PRESS UPS	1 Set to Failure
BENT OVER BARBELL ROW	1 Set to Failure

15. Saturday - Nutrition

Meal One

1 x multivitamin

- 2 Whole Eggs Boiled
- 2 slices of wholegrain toast with peanut butter

Quinoa Oats
- Add 1/4 cup of oats to water or almond milk
- 1 tbsp honey for sweetness.

NUTRITION FACTS
Calories: 561   Fat: 30.4 g Carbs: 16.2 g   Protein: 25.1g

Meal Two

Lean Shake
- 2 Scoops of 25 gram per scoop of Pea Protein Isolate.
- For a lean shake use water or mix with ½ cup of almond milk.

Meal Three

Vegan Platter
- Prepare 2 cups of Vegan cottage cheese (tofu based)
- Add a handful of Pumpkin seeds
- Serve with chick pea hummus and pitta bread

NUTRITION FACTS
Calories: 371   Fat: 33.2 g   Carbs: 17 g   Protein: 19.5 g

Meal Four

Quorn Burgers and Steamed Vegetables
- 10 ounce Quorn Burger Grilled
- Steamed Peas and Carrots on the side
- ¼ cup of buckwheat boiled
- Side of boiled/steamed Edamame beans

NUTRITION FACTS
Calories: 452   Fat: 34 g Carb: 18 g   Protein: 28 g

The Total Protein intake is 122.6 grams of protein. I would have 2 scoops of protein plus creatine after your workout making a grand total of 172.6.

This is a figure you can play with, add more, take away some etc.

16. Sunday - REST

So we've made it to our rest day - well done for an epic week of workouts!

So today is all about chilling, eating well, having your cheat meal - which is anything of your choice.

Meal One

1 x multivitamin

Vegan Breakfast
- 3-4 Whole eggs scrambled
- 2 x Quorn sausages
- ¼ cup baked beans
- 2 x Grilled tomatoes

NUTRITION FACTS
Calories: 461   Fat: 30.4 g   Carbs: 16.2 g   Protein: 37.1 g

Meal Two

Protein shake
- Add 2 Scoops of a 25 gram organic hemp protein
- Mix with water/almond milk or soy milk
- Add 1 banana

NUTRITION FACTS
Calories: 230   Fat: 20 g   Carbs: 10 g   Protein: 50 g

Meal Three

Cheat Meal!

Meal Four

Vegan Roast
- Add mixed vegetables (sweet potato, mushrooms, peppers, carrots)
- Sliced organic Tofu
- Add sliced red onions and seasoning then bake in the oven all together in a dish.

NUTRITION FACTS
Calories: 752   Fat: 29 g Carb: 16 g   Protein: 45 g

I'm not counting calories too much on a Sunday, have your favourite cheat meal and enjoy the rest!

17. Monday Week 2 - Back and Biceps

We are now entering Week 2 and it's time to get down to being a little more specific. I still want my big compound moves but we are going for detail this week.

If this is your first or second run at this, go light. Feel your muscles work with these new and old exercises.

Round 1

Exercise	Sets/Reps
PULL UP	1-2 sets of 15 reps (warm-up); 5 sets of 12, 10, 8, 6, 4 reps
Superset	
INCLINE BARBELL CURL	4 sets of 10-12 reps

Round 2

Exercise	Sets/Reps
CHEST SUPPORTED ROW	5 sets of 15, 12, 10, 8, 8 reps
Superset	
CHIN UP	4 sets of 10-12 reps

Round 3

Exercise	Sets/Reps
SEATED PULL DOWN	4 sets of 15, 12, 8, 6 reps
Superset	
SEATED CONCENTRATION CURL	4 sets of 12-10 rep

18. Monday Week 2 - Nutrition

Meal One

1 x multivitamin

1 x Whey Protein shake - with peanut butter and a banana

1 x Bowl of Granola

NUTRITION FACTS
Calories: 361   Fat: 18.4 g Carbs: 30.2 g Protein: 32.5 g

Meal Two

2 Scoops of 25 gram protein Whey Isolate shake

NUTRITION FACTS
Calories: 230   Fat: 20 g   Carbs: 10 g   Protein: 50 g

Meal Three

Pulses Salad Bowl
- Add Green salad leaves (try kale, spinach, rocket)
- Top with lentils, beans, pine nuts, peanut butter and vegan cheese.

NUTRITION FACTS
Calories: 471   Fat: 33.2 g   Carbs: 17 g   Protein: 18 g

Meal Four

Tofu steak and vegetables
- High protein Tofu steak grilled or BBQ
- Serve with brown rice or Quinoa

- Steam Broccoli and Cauliflower

NUTRITION FACTS
Calories: 452   Fat: 24 g Carb: 28 g   Protein: 22 g

The Total Protein intake is 122.5 grams of protein. I would have 2 scoops of protein plus creatine after your workout making a grand total of 172.5.

This is a figure you can play with, add more, take away some etc

19. Tuesday Week 2 - Abs and Rest

Before Breakfast:
20 x Crunches x 3
25 twists x 3 each side

Try to walk at least 6000 steps (use your phones pedometer) or for at least an hour.

Meal One

1 x multivitamin

1 x Whey Protein shake - with peanut butter and a banana

1 x Bowl of Granola

NUTRITION FACTS
Calories: 361   Fat: 18.4 g Carbs: 30.2 g Protein: 32.5 g

Meal Two

Lean Shake
- 2 Scoops of 25 gram per scoop of Pea Protein Isolate.
- For a lean shake use water or mix with ½ cup of almond milk.

Meal Three

Vegan Platter
- Prepare 2 cups of Vegan cottage cheese (tofu based)
- Add a handful of Pumpkin seeds
- Serve with chick pea hummus and pitta bread

NUTRITION FACTS
Calories: 371   Fat: 33.2 g   Carbs: 17 g   Protein: 19.5 g

Meal Four

Vegan Spinach Lasagne
- Use vegan cheese, organic spinach and serve with a side salad of fresh green leaves topped with balsamic vinegar

NUTRITION FACTS
Calories: 452   Fat: 34 g Carb: 38 g   Protein: 27 g

The Total Protein intake is 129 grams of protein. I would have 2 scoops of protein after your workout making a grand total of 179.

This is a figure you can play with, add more, take away some etc.

20. Wednesday Week 2 – Chest, Triceps and Shoulder

So we arrived at our Chest, Triceps and Shoulder workout, a great combo as we're working all the muscles which interconnect. Remember great form is key for both body parts. For chest presses imagine your biceps being bought closer together, your chest will do all the work.

If you're gassing after Chest and Triceps, consider splitting them up during the day. The early morning workout can be Chest and Tri's, early evening Shoulders. You then have Thursday as a full rest day.

Round 1

Exercise	Sets/Reps
INCLINE DUMBELL PRESS	1-2 sets of 15 reps (warm-up); 5 sets of 12, 10, 8, 6, 4 reps
Superset	
CLOSE GRIP FLAT BENCH PRESS	4 sets of 15, 12, 10, 8 reps

Round 2

Exercise	Sets/Reps
BARBELL BENCH PRESS	4 sets of 12, 10, 8, 6 reps
Superset	
CABLE OVERHEAD PRESS	4 sets of 15, 12, 10, 8 reps

Round 3

Exercise	Sets/Reps
DIPS	4 sets of 12, 10, 8, 6 reps
Superset	
CABLE PUSH DOWNS	4 sets of 15, 12, 8, 6 reps

Round 4

Exercise	Sets/Reps
HIGH TO LOW CABLE CROSS OVERS	4 sets of 12, 10, 8, 6 reps
Superset	
TRIANGLE PUSH UP	4 sets of 15, 12, 8, 6 reps

Shoulders

Make sure you are fully warmed up around the neck and shoulder area. Spend time looking each side, up, down and tilting your head. Warm those shoulders up with imaginary Peck Deck exercises.

Exercise	Sets/Reps
STANDING OVERHEARD PRESS	2 warm up light sets, 4 sets of 12, 10, 8, 8 reps
DUMBBELL LATERAL RAISES	4 sets of 15, 12, 10, 8 reps
REVERSE PECK DECK	4 sets of 8 reps

LYING FACE PULLS	3 sets of 10
STANDING OR KNEELING FACE PULLS	3 sets of 10

21. Wednesday Week 2 - Nutrition

Meal One

1 x multivitamin

Oats and Fresh Fruit
- 1/4 cup Quinoa oats with 1 tbsp. honey – use Almond Milk.
- Add blueberries and half a banana for a more filling and sweeter taste.

NUTRITION FACTS
Calories: 460   Fat: 10.4 g Carbs: 46.2 g Protein: 15.1 g

Meal Two

Lean Shake
- 2 Scoops of 25 gram per scoop of Pea Protein Isolate.
- For a lean shake use water or mix with ½ cup of almond milk.

Meal Three

Pea Soup
- Peas are boiled and blended with celery and vegetable stock sprinkled with vegan cheese.
- Rice and Black Beans

NUTRITION FACTS
Calories: 571   Fat: 13.2 g   Carbs: 37 g   Protein: 35 g

Meal Four

Tofu steak and vegetables
- High protein Tofu steak grilled or BBQ
- Serve with brown rice or Quinoa
- Steam Broccoli and Cauliflower

NUTRITION FACTS
Calories: 452   Fat: 24 g Carb: 28 g   Protein: 22 g

The Total Protein intake is 122.1 grams of protein. I would have 2 scoops of protein plus Creatine after your workout making a grand total of 172.1.

This is a figure you can play with, add more, take away some etc

22. Thursday Week 2 - Abs and Rest

Before Breakfast:
20 x Crunches x 3
25 twists x 3 each side

Try to walk at least 6000 steps (use your phones pedometer) or for at least an hour.

Meal One

- 3-4 Whole Eggs Boiled
- 2 Quorn sausages

Quinoa or gluten free oats
- 1/4 cup of oats with 1 tbsp. honey

NUTRITION FACTS
Calories: 361   Fat: 24.4 g Carbs: 36.2 g Protein: 36.1 g

Meal Two

2 Scoops of 25 gram protein Whey Isolate shake

NUTRITION FACTS
Calories: 230   Fat: 20 g   Carbs: 10 g   Protein: 50 g

Meal Three

Vegan Platter
- Prepare 2 cups of Vegan cottage cheese (tofu based)
- Add a handful of Pumpkin seeds
- Serve with chick pea hummus and pitta bread

NUTRITION FACTS
Calories: 371   Fat: 33.2 g   Carbs: 17 g   Protein: 19.5 g

Meal Four

Quorn Burgers and Steamed Vegetables
- 10 ounce Quorn Burger Grilled
- Steamed Peas and Carrots on the side
- ¼ cup of buckwheat boiled
- Side of boiled/steamed Edamame beans

NUTRITION FACTS
Calories: 452   Fat: 34 g Carb: 18 g   Protein: 28 g

The Total Protein intake is 182 grams of protein. I would have 2 scoops of protein plus creatine after your workout making a grand total of 241.

This is a figure you can play with, add more, take away some etc

23. Friday Week 2 - Legs and Calves

Make sure you warm up, lots of stretching. I especially make sure my neck is nice and warm, lots of looking to each side, tilting my head and looking up and down. I then like to make sure my shoulders are warm, windmills, light presses etc This area does a lot of heavy lifting and you don't want to pull anything.

Again as I stated if this is your first or second run at this, start light. Feel your muscles working with old and new exercises.

Round 1

Exercise	Sets/Reps
BARBELL SQUAT	2 warm up light sets, 4 sets of 12, 10, 8, 8 reps
FRONT SQUAT	4 sets of 15, 12, 10, 8 reps
ROMANIAN DEADLIFT	4 sets of 8 reps

Round 2

Exercise	Sets/Reps
BULGARIAN SPLIT SQUAT	3 sets of 12, 10, 8 reps
LEG CURLS	3 sets of 15, 12, 10 reps
HIP THRUSTS	3 sets of 10 reps

Round 3

Increase the weight little by little with each set.

Exercise	Sets/Reps
STANDING CALF RAISES	3 sets of 12, 10, 8 reps
SEATED CALF RAISE	3 sets of 12-15 reps

24. Friday Week 2 - Nutrition

Meal One

1 x multivitamin

Egg and Spinach Omelette
- 3-4 Whole Eggs whisked with a handful of organic spinach leaved loosely chopped and added to omelette
- Serve on a bed of fresh lettuce leaves (the greener the better)

Gluten Free Granola
- Granola with almond milk. Add fresh fruit and honey to taste.

NUTRITION FACTS
Calories: 461   Fat: 30.4 g Carbs: 16.2 g Protein: 34.1 g

Meal Two

Lean Shake
- 2 Scoops of 25 gram per scoop of Pea Protein Isolate.
- For a lean shake use water or mix with ½ cup of almond milk.

Meal Three

Pulses Salad Bowl
- Add Green salad leaves (try kale, spinach, rocket)
- Top with lentils, beans, pine nuts, peanut butter and vegan cheese.

NUTRITION FACTS
Calories: 471   Fat: 33.2 g   Carbs: 17 g   Protein: 18 g

Meal Four

Tofu steak and vegetables
- High protein Tofu steak grilled or BBQ
- Serve with brown rice or Quinoa
- Steam Broccoli and Cauliflower

NUTRITION FACTS
Calories: 452   Fat: 24 g Carb: 28 g   Protein: 22 g

The Total Protein intake is 124.1 grams of protein. I would have 2 scoops of protein plus creatine after your workout making a grand total of 174.1.

This is a figure you can play with, add more, take away some etc

25. Saturday Week 2 - Abs and Rest

Before Breakfast:
20 x Crunches x 3
25 twists x 3 each side

Aim to run for 30 minutes.

Meal One

- 3-4 Whole Eggs Boiled
- 2 Quorn sausages

Quinoa or gluten free oats
- 1/4 cup of oats with 1 tbsp. honey

NUTRITION FACTS
Calories: 361   Fat: 24.4 g Carbs: 36.2 g Protein: 36.1 g

Meal Two

- 2 Scoops of 25 gram Pea protein powder mixed with ½ cup of almond milk

NUTRITION FACTS
Calories: 230   Fat: 20 g   Carbs: 10 g   Protein: 50 g

Meal Three

Pulses Salad Bowl
- Add Green salad leaves (try kale, spinach, rocket)
- Top with lentils, beans, pine nuts, peanut butter and vegan cheese.

NUTRITION FACTS
Calories: 471   Fat: 33.2 g   Carbs: 17 g   Protein: 18 g

Meal Four

Vegan Spinach Lasagne
- Use vegan cheese, organic spinach and serve with a side salad of fresh green leaves topped with balsamic vinegar

NUTRITION FACTS
Calories: 452   Fat: 34 g Carb: 38 g   Protein: 27 g

The Total Protein intake is 131.1 grams of protein. I would have 2 scoops of protein plus Creatine after your workout making a grand total of 181.1.

This is a figure you can play with, add more, take away some etc.

26. Sunday - Rest

So we've made it to our rest day - well done for an epic workout!

So today is all about chilling, eating well, having your cheat meal - which is anything of your choice.

Meal One

1 x multivitamin

Vegan Breakfast
- 3-4 Whole eggs scrambled
- 2 x Quorn sausages
- ¼ cup baked beans
- 2 x Grilled tomatoes

NUTRITION FACTS
Calories: 461   Fat: 30.4 g   Carbs: 16.2 g   Protein: 37.1 g

Meal Two

Protein shake
- Add 2 Scoops of a 25 gram organic hemp protein
- Mix with water/almond milk or soy milk
- Add 1 banana

NUTRITION FACTS
Calories: 230   Fat: 20 g   Carbs: 10 g   Protein: 50 g

Meal Three

Cheat Meal!

Meal Four

Vegan Roast
- Add mixed vegetables (sweet potato, mushrooms, peppers, carrots)
- Sliced organic Tofu
- Add sliced red onions and seasoning then bake in the oven all together in a dish.

NUTRITION FACTS
Calories: 752   Fat: 29 g Carb: 16 g   Protein: 45 g

I'm not counting calories too much on a Sunday, have your favourite cheat meal and enjoy the rest!

27. Final Notes and Cheats

So we have reached the end of the 2 week training routine and your muscles should be aching. This is a good thing!

You may need to adjust your nutrition adding more protein, adding more carbs after training if you're feeling low energy. Remember if you don't fuel your workouts and yourself when you're not working out properly, you won't make the maximal progress.

In terms of training you may struggle at first. I would reduce sets - not workouts. Keep to the schedule, keep working the muscles regularly and you will get results.

There are a number of cheats I use to maximize muscles gain in terms of supplements.

- A Pre and Post workout shake is a given - 25grams minimum. I've taken this into account in the nutrition, 1 x shake before and 1 x after, both 25 grams.

- Creatine is a great as a post workout and fantastic to add muscle size:

  Most creatine is synthetically created and 100% vegan. Capsules can however contain gelatine. Ask your specific supplier if you're uncertain.

  Taking creatine's no problem for your liver or kidneys. Unless you have an kidney injury or high risk of developing kidney problems (diabetes for example).

No other variant has proven to be more beneficial than creatine monohydrate (including creatine magnesium chelate, creatine pyruvate, creatine citrate, creapure (micronized creatine), buffered creatine (kre-alkalyn), creatine hydrochloride (con-cret), creatine hydrochloride, creatine ethyl ester).

- Fast-digesting carbs are also essential - oats and a large dollop of honey. Even an oatabix with honey. Or a carb drink like Waxy-maize.

How to Raise Testosterone Naturally:

1) Stay within 8-15% bodyfat
2) Intake a good source of Zinc: beans, chickpeas, lentils, tofu, walnuts, cashew nuts, chia seeds, ground linseed, hemp seeds, pumpkin seeds, wholemeal bread and quinoa. Ensure that your daily diet contains plenty of zinc-rich foods.
3) Intake a good source of Vitamin D: Maitake, Morel, Chanterelle, Shiitake, Alfalfa, Fortified cereal, Lichens, Vegan D3 supplements
4) Get at least 8 hours of restful sleep

So there we have it - have a go and enjoy the workouts!

If you'd like some more brilliant Vegetarian food options here:

Vegetarian Bodybuilding Nutrition: How To Crack The Muscle Building Success Code With Vegetarian Bodybuilding Nutrition

Additional Training Books:

Want a Brand New Way to create Massive Growth and really hit those Arms:
https://www.amazon.com/dp/1542995418

Want a new style of training boulder-sized Shoulders:
https://www.createspace.com/6954466

All the best guys
M

Made in the USA
Middletown, DE
20 September 2023